CONTENTS

KU-370-027

LEVEL UP IN REAL LIFE

1

Maybe you've heard that people who play video games are lazy. They stare at screens all day, their brains turn to mush, and they never see the sun. Luckily, research shows this isn't true.

Scientists interested in learning about video games have made many discoveries. With each new study, their research reveals more about how video games affect our lives. Scientists have learned that video games are not as bad as people say. Video games can even be good for you!

VIDEO GAMES ARE GOOD FOR YOU!

by Daniel Mauleón

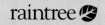
raintree

a Capstone company — publishers for children

Raintree is an imprint of Capstone Global Library Limited, a company incorporated in England and Wales having its registered office at 264 Banbury Road, Oxford, OX2 7DY – Registered company number: 6695582

www.raintree.co.uk
myorders@raintree.co.uk

Editor: Gena Chester
Designers: Kay Fraser and Rachel Tesch
Media researcher: Tracy Cummins
Original illustrations © Capstone Global Library Limited 2020
Production Specialist: Kathy McColley
Originated by Capstone Global Library Ltd
Printed and bound in India

ISBN 978 1 4747 8810 6 (hardback)
ISBN 978 1 4747 8816 8 (paperback)

British Library Cataloguing in Publication Data
A full catalogue record for this book is available from the British Library.

Acknowledgements
We would like to thank the following for permission to reproduce photographs: Getty Images: Yamaguchi Haruyoshi/Sygma, 14; iStockphoto: mariusFM77, 13; Newscom: REUTERS/Matthew Tostevin, 26; Shutterstock: Anna Chernova, Design Element, Anton27, 7, Arieliona, 10, aurielaki, Cover, 1, Barone Firenze, 23, Christos Georghiou, Design Element, defotoberg, 9, Denys Prykhodov, 16, Designworkz, Design Element, Elena Schweitzer, 19, fizkes, 21, LightField Studios, 5, 29, VectorPixelStar, Design Element, Yes I Shoot models, 25, yurakr, Design Element.

Every effort has been made to contact copyright holders of material reproduced in this book. Any omissions will be rectified in subsequent printings if notice is given to the publisher.

All the internet addresses (URLs) given in this book were valid at the time of going to press. However, due to the dynamic nature of the internet, some addresses may have changed, or sites may have changed or ceased to exist since publication. While the author and publisher regret any inconvenience this may cause readers, no responsibility for any such changes can be accepted by either the author or the publisher.

CORRELATION AND CAUSATION

Good studies show the difference between correlation and causation. These two maths words may sound similar, but if mixed up, they can lead to the wrong information. *Correlation* means two things are connected. *Causation* means one thing affected another.

FACT!

A 2019 survey in the UK found that 42 per cent of British people aged between 55 and 64 have played video games in the last five years.

GIVE YOUR BRAIN A BOOST

Video games are good at **motivating** players to complete tasks and overcome challenges. If you play games, you already know it feels good to finish a level. Whether you earn a victory royale or race your way to first place, understanding why games are good at motivating players is important.

dopamine a brain chemical that relays information; dopamine helps control movement, attention, learning and emotional responses

motivate something that encourages a person to do a task

That feeling where you want to keep playing comes from a chemical in the brain called **dopamine**. Your brain releases dopamine when you achieve something and when you get close to completing a task. This is why you want to try again after coming second. You feel victory is just around the corner.

By activating dopamine in your brain, video games motivate you to keep playing. This can make tasks that are difficult more exciting. It also encourages players to focus, try new ideas and learn. Plus, gamers may connect the success of beating a challenge to other challenges in their lives.

FACT!

In the original *Super Mario Bros.* game, players who finished a level at a certain time were rewarded with fireworks. The victory and special effects added to the players' enjoyment.

ACTION-PACKED . . .
PATTERN FINDING?

When you learn something new, you train your brain to find new connections. Your brain then works through these connections to create new patterns. A team of researchers from the University of Rochester, New York, USA, wanted to see if video games could help with learning.

They experimented with two groups of people. One group played *Call of Duty* and other action games. The other group played non-action video games, such as *The Sims*. They played 50 hours over nine weeks. Researchers then tested the groups' abilities to find patterns. The group that played action games performed better on the pattern task. But the action games didn't directly teach players how to find patterns. Researchers believe high-action game play trained the group to think quickly and try new things.

Researchers tested the players several months later. The action-gaming group still did better than the other group, suggesting the training gained by high-action games had a long-lasting effect.

VIDEO GAMES AND STRESS RELIEF

Have you noticed that video games help clear your brain after a long day at school? A study suggests that adding gaming to your end-of-day routine could be a good idea.

Scientists know that mentally recovering from a day of work is important. Recovery prepares you for the next day and prevents you from feeling stressed. Researchers at the University College London Interaction Centre studied the relationship between gaming and recovery. They found that the number of hours spent playing digital games had a positive correlation to how well players recovered. This study suggests that people who take time to enjoy hobbies are more likely to recover from work.

GET A MOVE ON

Not all games are made for the couch. Motion controls have helped spur a rise in movement-based games. By using global positioning systems (GPS) in phones, games such as *Pokémon Go* get players out of the house. Playing active games encourages exercise, leading to many health benefits.

If you exercise during the day, you may notice it's easier to get a full night's rest. Exercise also releases brain chemicals called endorphins to boost your mood. It may seem backward, but exercise also gives you more energy.

The Wii console, *Wii Fit* game and Balance Board

FACT!
Released in 2008, *Wii Fit* was a video game designed to improve players' health. It featured the *Wii Fit* Balance Board, which tracked players' movements as they did yoga, stretched or played other games.

FANCY FOOTWORK

There is no denying that dancing is good for you. Whether in a ballroom or your living room, it can be great for your health. Dancing gives your muscles a workout and boosts the strength of your heart and lungs. Dancing video games give these same benefits to players.

A teen playing *Dance Dance Revolution*

FACT!
Since the first *Just Dance* came out in 2009, there have been more than 20 versions, including *Just Dance: Disney Party* and *Just Dance: Kids*.

Just Dance is a popular dancing game series. Once the music starts, players match the moves on the screen. *Just Dance* keeps score using motion controllers, or motion-tracking cameras. The closer you match the move, the higher your score. Later versions of *Just Dance* let people connect with a smartphone. The bright lights and sound effects let you know when you are doing well and encourage you to keep dancing.

Join the revolution

Before *Just Dance* arrived, players grooved to the 1998 **arcade** game *Dance Dance Revolution*, or *DDR*. In *DDR*, players used their feet to step on four large buttons. The buttons matched arrows on a large screen. The on-screen arrows zipped past to the beat of the music. Instead of following dance moves, players needed to step on the button matching the correct direction in time with the music. Hopping quickly from button to button proved challenging for some players. The better your timing, the better you scored. Eventually fans bought portable dance pads to play *DDR* on their home consoles. Even though *Just Dance* has taken over, you can still find *DDR* machines in some arcades. There are even large tournaments where players show off their moves.

arcade a place people go to play coin-operated games

HOW *POKÉMON GO* GOT THE WORLD WALKING

When *Pokémon Go* launched in the summer of 2016, people got moving. By using their smartphones, children and adults could explore their real surroundings in search of hidden Pokémon.

The mobile game used **augmented reality**, or AR. It paired the best-selling video game *Pokémon* with the real world. *Pokémon Go* was an overnight hit. Parks around the world were filled with gamers of all ages hunting for Pokémon to capture.

FACT!
In 2016 *Pokémon Go* launched its Apple Watch app.

Soon after the game launched, developers from two fitness **apps** noticed differences in user behaviour. Cardiogram is an app that tracks heart rate and exercise on Apple watches. The app found that more users were exercising at least 30 minutes a day. Another fitness tracker called Jawbone noticed similar results. Jawbone reported a 62.5 per cent increase in steps by users who mentioned *Pokémon Go* on the app. The fitness app creators couldn't prove it was *Pokémon Go* that made the difference, but it seemed the likely cause.

app a useful program that is downloaded to computers and mobile devices; app is short for application

augmented reality an enhanced view of your surroundings that have been added to digitally

As players tracked down Pikachu in their gardens, researchers started tracking players. The American Heart Association reported that *Pokémon Go* users were twice as likely to reach 10,000 daily steps. A study from Duke University, North Carolina, USA, asked iPhone users to report daily step counts. They found that *Pokémon Go* players walked an average of 2,000 steps more than people who didn't play it.

Another study by the City of London University in 2017 found that players were walking more than ever, often choosing to walk to work instead of taking the bus. A number of players with physical disabilities reported that they were more active than they had been previously. These kinds of games will likely keep players walking, connecting and catching Pokémon together for years to come.

FACT!

Since the launch of *Pokémon Go* (shown in the photo above), other AR games have been created. In *Jurassic World Alive* players search for prehistoric dinosaurs instead of Pokémon.

YOUR PRESCRIPTION: MORE VIDEO GAMES

Playing movement-based games can do more than help you stay healthy. Some researchers and physical therapists are learning how it can help people recover from serious injuries. **Virtual reality**, or VR, is the next big trend in video games. Developers at VirZOOM are creating new games and experiences that use VR to promote healthy gaming. For it to work, players need a VR headset and a special exercise bike. In the virtual world, they can ride a horse, fly on a Pegasus or drive a tank. In the real world, they pedal a bike.

Companies such as Samsung are spending time learning about the benefits of VR for reducing patient pain. In a recent study, they found that experiencing nature videos through VR greatly lowered pain.

virtual reality a realistic 3D world drawn by a computer that can be seen using a special headset

The company Nero Rehab VR uses virtual reality to help with individual patient needs, such as brain or physical therapy. The company creates doctor-approved VR exercises. Because therapy is happening in virtual reality, patients tend to forget their real-world limits. This helps them to reach their therapy goals faster. Eventually Nero Rehab VR hopes to bring its exercises to patient homes, making it more affordable and accessible.

FACT!
Another Samsung study found that VR decreases pain in patients by 52 per cent.

EXERGAMES

The company MIRA uses physical therapy software and focuses on making patient recovery manageable. The centre developed exercise games called Exergames. Exergames were built around physical therapy. MIRA's system uses a Microsoft Kinect connected to a camera. The Kinect uses cameras to track patient movement and control the game. These games make physical therapy fun, speedy and easy.

Patients play different Exergames depending on what muscles they need to move. Because the therapy takes place in a game, patients are more likely to finish their whole routine.

amblyopia a medical term for when the vision in one eye is reduced because the eye and the brain are not working together properly
disorder a mental or physical condition

Exercising for your eyes?

The Research Institute of the McGill University Health Centre in Montreal, Canada, found that a special version of *Tetris* can improve an eye **disorder** called **amblyopia**. This condition is also known as lazy eye. *Tetris* players have to stack moving blocks. Researchers made people with amblyopia play while wearing a headset. One eye could see the blocks that were moving. The other eye could see the blocks that were already placed. Players had to use information from both eyes to succeed. This set-up made a player's eyes and brain work together to play the game, which improved the weakened eye.

MAKE FRIENDS THROUGH VIDEO GAMES

4

Close friendships improve your mood by boosting happiness and lowering stress. Friends can make you feel good about who you are by boosting your self-confidence. Positive friendships can make life easier when things get tough. Friends can encourage positive health choices, and people with close friends are less likely to have serious health problems.

A great way to make friends is by playing video games together. Whether online or in person, playing games can provide a sense of community. Plus, when friends play games together, they also learn good life skills.

FACT!

A study done by the University of California, USA, showed that online friendships can be just as meaningful as face-to-face ones.

In *Minecraft*, players can build worlds and friendships.

TAKE CHARGE

Nearly 70 per cent of gamers play with others in the same room. About 30 per cent play with others through the internet. Some new friendships are built in online worlds. In *Minecraft*, gamers use blocks and creativity to build their own worlds. While playing together, gamers have to agree, solve problems and learn together in order to create successfully. They learn who to trust and how to be a good leader. These skills can transfer into the real world when working with others. Young people with good social skills are more likely to have high self-esteem and do better in school.

FACT!

In *Fortnite: Save The World*, players battle against monsters. Working in teams of four, they build forts and use gear to fight monsters and complete missions.

VIDEO GAMES ARE GOOD FOR YOU

Research into video games is still new, especially when it comes to new technology like handheld systems and virtual reality. However, studies already show that video games definitely have benefits. From boosting your brain to making you a better team player, video games do a lot of good for players. Researchers continue to learn more about video games, especially as games become more popular. The long-term effects of video games on lifelong players are still unknown. Most importantly, video games should be enjoyed in **moderation**. With that in mind, what will you play next?

moderation in a way that is reasonable and not extreme or too much

Glossary

amblyopia a medical term for when the vision in one eye is reduced because the eye and the brain are not working together properly

app a useful program that is downloaded to computers and mobile devices; app is short for application

arcade a place people go to play coin-operated games

augmented reality an enhanced view of your surroundings that have been added to digitally

disorder a mental or physical condition

dopamine a brain chemical that relays information; dopamine helps control movement, attention, learning and emotional responses

moderation in a way that is reasonable and not extreme or too much

motivate something that encourages a person to do a task

virtual reality a realistic 3D world drawn by a computer that can be seen using a special headset

Find out more

Coding Games from Scratch (Code it Yourself), Rachel Ziter (Raintree, 2018)

Computer Games Designer (The Coolest Jobs on the Planet), Mark Featherstone (Raintree, 2014)

STEAM Jobs for Gamers (STEAM Jobs), Sam Rhodes (Raintree, 2018)

Video Game Trivia: What You Never Knew about Popular Games, Design Secrets and the Coolest Characters (Not Your Ordinary Trivia), Sean McCollum (Raintree, 2018)

Websites

Learn How to Make Video Games
studio.code.org/courses

Thought-Provoking Non-violent Games
www.commonsensemedia.org/lists/thought-provoking-nonviolent-games-for-tweens-and-teens

Why Video Games Can be Good for You
www.gamedesigning.org/why-video-games-are-good/

Index